Made in the USA
Monee, IL
16 March 2022

92967832R00057